Au...

Fredah I. Agbeje

**Introduction to Internet Security for PHP Web Developers**

Audu Jonathan Adoga
Fredah I. Agbeje

# Introduction to Internet Security for PHP Web Developers

## PHP Security

**LAP LAMBERT Academic Publishing**

**Impressum / Imprint**

Bibliografische Information der Deutschen Nationalbibliothek: Die Deutsche Nationalbibliothek verzeichnet diese Publikation in der Deutschen Nationalbibliografie; detaillierte bibliografische Daten sind im Internet über http://dnb.d-nb.de abrufbar.
Alle in diesem Buch genannten Marken und Produktnamen unterliegen warenzeichen-, marken- oder patentrechtlichem Schutz bzw. sind Warenzeichen oder eingetragene Warenzeichen der jeweiligen Inhaber. Die Wiedergabe von Marken, Produktnamen, Gebrauchsnamen, Handelsnamen, Warenbezeichnungen u.s.w. in diesem Werk berechtigt auch ohne besondere Kennzeichnung nicht zu der Annahme, dass solche Namen im Sinne der Warenzeichen- und Markenschutzgesetzgebung als frei zu betrachten wären und daher von jedermann benutzt werden dürften.

Bibliographic information published by the Deutsche Nationalbibliothek: The Deutsche Nationalbibliothek lists this publication in the Deutsche Nationalbibliografie; detailed bibliographic data are available in the Internet at http://dnb.d-nb.de.
Any brand names and product names mentioned in this book are subject to trademark, brand or patent protection and are trademarks or registered trademarks of their respective holders. The use of brand names, product names, common names, trade names, product descriptions etc. even without a particular marking in this works is in no way to be construed to mean that such names may be regarded as unrestricted in respect of trademark and brand protection legislation and could thus be used by anyone.

Coverbild / Cover image: www.ingimage.com

Verlag / Publisher:
LAP LAMBERT Academic Publishing
ist ein Imprint der / is a trademark of
OmniScriptum GmbH & Co. KG
Heinrich-Böcking-Str. 6-8, 66121 Saarbrücken, Deutschland / Germany
Email: info@lap-publishing.com

Herstellung: siehe letzte Seite /
Printed at: see last page
**ISBN: 978-3-659-59574-5**

Zugl. / Approved by: Cambridge,Anglia Ruskin University,Diss.,2013

# Preface

The purpose of this book is not to teach a novice how to develop PHP applications but, it creates awareness and serves as a security reference point for beginners who are only inquisitive about writing codes without considering common vulnerabilities that could emanate from such codes. Though the awareness is presented starting from history, it is a deliberate action to give you a solid background on some very important aspects of software security that most computer professionals think are negligible. It may interest you to know that updating your software to a stable version is a very important security measure that has been neglected.

The first chapter explains how PHP can work together with other languages when developing web applications. It also sheds light on what motivated the authors to write this book. The chapter also presents the work of some researchers and the weaknesses observed from such works.

Chapter two gives brief histories of HTML, SQL and that of PHP. It also presents detail explanations on how to upgrade these languages to higher and stable versions. Some attacks and vulnerabilities on web applications have been discussed in this chapter. It also gives insight on how to prevent XSS injection, SQL injection and some secure coding practices that are related to so many aspects of Web Development.

If you have a PHP website to develop, how are you supposed to start? Some ways of doing it based on our experience have been discussed in this chapter (chapter 3). This will help in achieving the desired security level and for this reason a fictitious web portal is used in this work for better understanding of various security concepts.

The last chapter completes the test plan that was prepared in chapter 3, and some practical code segments presented pictorially in order to make a beginner have better understanding of some security concepts such as the use of injection prevention codes, the use of mysqli or PDO for connection to database, crypt password hashing with salt and the use of utf8 character encoding.

1

# Contents

# 1 Chapter 1 General Introduction

## 1.1 Introduction

The security of PHP and other compatible languages on the internet are issues of serious concern to the PHP community at present. A secure system is a system that is devoid of flaws or security holes while vulnerability is defined as a flaw that causes a software system to work contrary to the purpose that it was designed for and could be exploited by fraudulent users (OIS, 2004).

PHP, HTML, CSS, and MySQL can work together perfectly as a secure system on the internet. PHP is the most common server-side scripting language and over 70% of web servers deploy this but the challenge is this: other competitors such as ASPX or JSP developers enjoy in-built security programs in such languages but, PHP is left with a lot of flaws (OWASP, 2013). This triggers the need for a deliberate action to ameliorate this problem.

This book is motivated by the fact that, over the years, software vulnerabilities have increased at an alarming rate. One thousand ninety (1,090) vulnerabilities were discovered in the year 2000 but, after few years (2006), eight thousand sixty four (8,064) new flaws were discovered (CERT, 2009). From 1995 to 2008, forty four thousand seventy four (44,074) flaws were reported (CERT, 2000).

Software vulnerabilities have led to series of tragedies: accounts are constantly being attacked due to broken authentication and session management. Privileges are being taken over from the real owners, forgery of victims' identities and redirection of users to wrong sites is on the increase (OWASP, 2013). More threats keep coming due to improper programming principles such as wrong escaping of untrusted data, misconfiguration of applications and inaccurate frameworks, libraries and plugins. This is not good for the software development industry.

However, there are a lot of practices that are good to follow when it comes to developing secure applications. This book sees the need to carefully study those practices and recommend them for software developers, especially the beginners in software development.

## 1.2 Some Research Works on PHP Security Flaws

Several research works have been conducted on PHP security: a research was conducted to detect vulnerabilities in web applications using static analysis tool called Pixy. The tool was able to discover 15 unknown PHP flaws from three web applications but they were all cross-side scripting vulnerabilities (Javonovic, Kruegel and Kirda, 2006).

In another research conducted by (Vieira, Antunes and Madeira, 2009), 300 web services were evaluated for flaws using four recognized scanners. Several security holes were discovered but these tools also had limitations. There were differences in the flaws detected and furthermore, the number of false-positive was 40% and 35% in two situations. This is high and unacceptable. Some scanners were also observed to have low coverage (two scanners had less than 20%). This is also unacceptable.

Moreover, (Yoshioka, Washizaki and Maruyama, 2008) conducted a security patterns survey. The study sheds light on the use of pattern at every stage of software development but failed to produce a working model that could be used as reference point during development of a secured site.

# 2    Chapter 2    History and Update

## 2.1    Hypertext Mark-up Language and the Web

According to Longman (1998), Hypertext Mark-up Language (HTML), the language of the web used today either directly or indirectly, is a result of the work of Tim Berners-Lee who wrote the prototype in 1992. He continued the work after 1992 and invented the web in 1989 with HTML as its language. The World Wide Web started at the European Laboratory for Particle Physics (CERN), a place that no one thought such invention could be possible. Before this invention, there was a similar invention by an Apple Computer programmer (Bill Atkinson) in the late 1980s called HyperCard which drew the attention of many but had limitation. The hypertext links could only jump from one document to another on the same computer. The links could not work globally so, it became a matter of concern.

### 2.1.1 The Domain Name

Before the coming of domain name in the middle of 1980s, people were using IP addresses for communication but because it was not user-friendly, the issue of domain name came up. Distributed Name Service was invented and it could map domain names with IP addresses. This was very innovative for those that did not want to pass through the rigours of IP addresses.

### 2.1.2 Tim Berners-Lee's HTML was based on SGML (Standard Generalized Mark-up Language).

Berners-Lee's invention of HTML was a good idea to follow because it was based on SGML, an internationally accepted standard for making text into various formats such as paragraphs, heading and title. Hypertext links were also compatible with most systems such as Macintoshes, personal computers and UNIX systems that were connected to the Internet at that time. Another advantage was being browser independent. A System of protocol called hypertext Transfer Protocol was also developed by him for easy retrieval of hypertext documents through hypertext links.

### 2.1.3 HTML+ and Mosaic

In September 1991, a mailing list called www-talk was introduced which made online sharing of ideas possible. This drew the attention of researchers from various institutions and as a result of this, Dave Ragget, a Hewllet Packard worker in England visited Tim in 1992 to discuss making HTML a better one for consumption on a large scale. When Ragget returned to England, he was able to develop a better version of HTML called HTML+.

Furthermore, the popularity of this invention continued to increase and by 1992, a browser called mosaic was developed at the University of Illinois in a research centre called National Centre for Supercomputer Applications (NCSA) and by 1993 in the month of April, the first version was released to Sun Microsystems' workstation

## 2.1.4 The Image Tag

There was a debate in a www-talk group the insertion of images in HTML documents. Notable amongst the members were Dan Connolly, Tim Berners-Lee, Dave Ragget and Marc Andreessen. The image tag by Mosaic team was presented by Marc Andreessen and it was implemented in HTML but with the coming of HTML4, the OBJECT tag has the qualities of replacing the IMG tag.

## 2.1.5 The Arena browser

Dave Ragget saw the need to work on the development of a browser called Arena. He did it alone because there was no support from companies. Most of them could not belief that the Internet would be a success. The issue of making money from the Internet was not clear to so many companies. Some people also misunderstood Internet to be meant for the people in academics. Dave observed that there was no enough time for him to finish what he had started so, his dining room was partly used as a laboratory. He was able to demonstrate his work in a World Wide Web conference organized in Geneva in 1994. The browser was later used by CERN.

## 2.1.6 The Release of Hypertext Mark-up Language 2

As at 1993 and 1994, So many browsers have added new features to HTML. This was a great problem because the companies involved were not strictly following a particular standard. Based on these variations, Dan Connolly and his colleagues saw the need for uniformity so all the HTML tags from various sources were collected to form one draft document named as HTML 2 by Tim Berners-Lee. The draft document was then sent to the internet community for comments. Dan also wrote an exact definition of the language.

## 2.1.7 The formation of the WWW Consortium

The World Wide Web consortium was formed in 1997 by some of the best members of the Internet community led by Tim Berners-Lee with the aim of developing standards. Countries like the United States, Japan and France served as bases for the consortium and renowned companies such as Netscape Communications Corporations, Microsoft Corporations, Hewlett Packard, among many others supported the group.

## 2.1.8 HTML 3.2

In 1995, so many types of HTML documents came up but there was the need to separate document definition from style. This was emphasized by the academic community. Issues like background colour, text colour and font size were said to be beyond the scope of HTML. Dave Ragget brought his new idea about HTML (HTML 3) in a write-up called Internet draft: the draft included all HTML features, new tags and style support was also included. The addition of so many new features in this draft made it difficult for the International Engineering Task Force to ratify though so many companies started implementing it using their browsers with some limitations. In a meeting of IETF in 1995, HTML table was included in the draft and HTML 3 draft was changed to HTML 3.2 draft.

## 2.1.9 A Change from IETF HTML to ERB HTML

Due to failure on the side of IETF, the group work was closed. They could not coordinate the work saddled on them effectively. The browser differences on HTML implementation kept increasing. This was a problem to standardization, hence the formation of an HTML Editorial Review Board (ERB) to help with issues of standard. Problems such as that of MARQUE from Microsoft and blink tag from Netscape were solved by ERB HTML. This brought sanity and respect for the standard. A draft for scripting was also written by Dave Ragget.

In 1998, a new standard called HTML 4.0 came up but there were problems. No browser could completely implement it. The OBJECT also works differently in different browsers. The WHAT WG and the W3C then worked together and released HTML5 which was a very good standard for the present internet.

## 2.2   Hypertext Processor (PHP)

## 2.2.1 PHP 2.0

According to (PHP, 2013), PHP was originally called PHP/FI when Rasmus Lerdorf created it in 1994. Lerdorf, used C programming language to develop binaries of Common Gateway Interface. The set of binaries was used by Lerdorf to track visitation to his internet resume. He gave the suit of script name that is commonly called PHP Tools.

More functionality were later added to PHP Tools based on the needs of that time and PHP was able to interact with database and he was able to make PHP a framework upon which other software developers could use to develop dynamic websites. The source code for PHP was made known to the public in June, 1995. This resulted to great improvement in the language because developers could modify the source code to give them what they want. They could also provide solution in form of patches to the source code.

In September of 1995, Lerdorf did more work on PHP and changed the name to FI meaning Forms Interpreter: FI had the basic qualities of PHP. It was like Perl in terms of the variables used and could embed HTML syntax. This version enjoyed a lot of popularity from developers from all over the world but a complete rewrite of FI was done in October of 1995 and the name was changed to " Personal Home Page Construction Kit " . This was regarded as an advanced scripting interface that was easy for C and Perl programmers to adopt though it was only compatible with POSIX and UNIX.

In 1996, there was a complete rewrite of the whole program that led to an evolution of a readopted name PHP/FI. This was more of a programming language than a mere set of tools that was previously used because; there were built-in capabilities for databases, cookies and functions that were defined by users. By 1997, PHP/FI had moved out of beta stage and continued to enjoy great popularity with PHP 2.0 version but was full of limitations due to its one-man major developer nature and minor contributors.

## 2.2.2    PHP 3.0

Zeev Suraski of Tel Aviv, Israel and Andi Gutmans were trying to develop an e-commerce application for a university in 1997 but discovered that PHP/FI was limited so they collaborated with Lerdoft and developed a completely independent version of PHP and named it PHP 3.0. This version was announced in June 1998 but before the announcement, so many developers already installed it in their systems all over the world. This version was better than PHP/FI in so many ways:

a)    It overcame the problem of limited personal use.
b)    It was an extensible language.

9

c)   It supported multiple protocols, databases and application programming interfaces.

d)   It could be installed on windows and Macintosh.

e)   It had support for object-oriented programming.

### 2.2.3   PHP 4.0

Immediately after the release of PHP 3.0 Zeev and Andi started work on PHP 4.0 that led to its official release on May 2000. The new development came with an engine called Zend. PHP4.0 was to be more efficient than PHP 3.0. It could work with many more servers. This version was also able to support HTTP sessions. So many language constructs were added to the language. Attention was also given to security since a more secure user input method was introduced.

### 2.2.4   PHP 5.0

A new version of PHP called PHP 5.0 was made known officially to the public in the year 2004. This version derived its strength from dozens of developers' team all over World, its powerful zend engine 2.0 and. A lot of new features and support for object model were added to this release.

PHP 5 was released in July 2004 after long development and several pre-releases. It is mainly driven by its core, the *Zend Engine 2.0* with a new object model and dozens of other new features.

PHP's development team includes dozens of developers, as well as dozens of others working on PHP-related and supporting projects, such as PEAR, PECL, and documentation, and an underlying network infrastructure of well over one-hundred individual web servers on six of the seven continents of the world. Though only an estimate based upon statistics from previous years, it is safe to presume PHP is now installed on tens or even perhaps hundreds of millions of domains around the world.

## 2.3   MySQL

### 2.3.1 MySQL and the MySQL Server

Based on a historical account by MySQL (2013), MySQL is the most popular among the open source database management system (DBMS). All the benefits derived from MySQL are as a result of philanthropic work of Oracle Corporation. Anything from simple database to a complex one could be done through MySQL. For one to add data or delete data or process data or restructure data in an acceptable format, the importance of a relational database management system such as MySQL cannot be overemphasized.

Moreover, organising data into tables that work together in a database is one of the potent factors to consider if a database management system is said to be a relational one. With MySQL, data could be organized into tables, with rows and columns, unique relationships of many to many or one to many or many to one and so on. MySQL server could work together alone or together with other applications either at the back end or the front end. This makes MySQL a compatible and a highly acceptable open source database management system. The SQL part of the MySQL means "Structured Query Language" and the responsibility of defining the language is saddled on ANSI/ISO standard that has been in existence since 1986.

In addition, one could download and use the MySQL software free. The modification of the code by programmers is also allowed. This is why it is called open source software. MySQL server is very reliable and fast software that could be used on laptops and desktops together with other applications. The server could be adjusted to take the advantage of the computer's CPU to increase its speed. It can work effectively in a network environment and in a highly demanding condition. MySQL software is client/server software that is compatible with a wide range of applications at both back and front end. It is very compatible with so many application programming interfaces (APIs). MySQL is pronounced "My Ess Que Ell", officially. Though, it is allowed to be pronounced in some other ways.

## 2.3.2 MySQL Development

MySQL started with an idea of using an existing database management system called MSQL to connect to tables but was found to be slow and not flexible. This led to the development of an SQL interface called MySQL.

Monty Widenius was one of the founders of MySQL and he had a daughter called "My", so MySQL was named after her. The dolphin that appears on MySQL website ( http://dev.mysql.com ) is called "Sakila". The name was given after series of names suggested by MySQL users. The one suggested by Ambrose Twebaze, an African from Uganda was chosen. Sakila is said to be a female name that originated from Siswate, one of the languages of Swaziland. Twebaze was a software developer (open source) at that time. Table 2.1 below shows how MySQL moves from one version to another with additional functionality.

| Feature | MySQL Series |
|---|---|
| Unions | 4.0 |
| Subqueries | 4.1 |
| R-trees | 4.1 (for myisam storage engine) |
| Stored procedures and functions | 5.0 |
| Views | 5.0 |
| Cursors | 5.0 |
| XA transactions | 5.0 |
| Triggers | 5.0 and 5.1 |
| Event Scheduler | 5.1 |
| Partitioning | 5.1 |
| Pluggable storage engine API | 5.1 |
| Plugin API | 5.1 |
| InnoDB plugin | 5.1 |
| Row-based replication | 5.1 |
| Server log tables | 5.1 |

Table 2.1: Features and MySQL Series that come with them

Source: MySQL (2013), MySQL Development History

MySQL 5.1 was made known to the public in as MySQL 5.1.30 in 2008. MySQL 5.0 was made public for commercials in 2005 as MySQL 5.0.15. MySQL (2013) further said that henceforth, only patches to security holes will be made to 5.0 and MySQL 5.1 and the older version and only critical patches will be made to the lower versions of 5.1 and 5.0.

## 2.3.3 Upgrading MySQL

For someone to upgrade from MySQL 5.0 to 5.0.10 or any version that came after this, one must upgrade his/her grant tables. Though MySQL will try to protect your data, it is of outmost importance to always back up data before installing new software.

Also, to upgrade from any version that came before MySQL 5.0 to MySQL 5.0, it is a good practice to use mysqldump to drop tables before upgrading. To move from one release to another, you must not skip one version. Upgrade in the order of their releases until you reach the desired version. For example, if you want to upgrade from MySQL 4.0 to MySQL 5.0, you have to upgrade first to 4.1 then finally to 5.0. Mysqldump or mysqlhotcopy could be used for backups but mysqldump is more acceptable because it can give you correct backups of various tables.

## 2.3.4 Things that were added to MySQL 5.0

Some of the features added to MySQL 5.0 are:

(a)   You can use instance manager to stop or start the server
(b)   Greater accuracy for mathematical values through the introduction of a library for fixed-point Arithmetic.
(c)   Storage engines such as archive and federated were added.
(d)   More power for handling transactions and the introduction of a storage format that could save up to 20% of memory space that was required by previous versions of InnoDB . MySQL was able to support a transaction type called Distributed transactions for InnoDB. The ability to manage multiple transactions from different sources and such transactions are either complete or they are rolled back.
(e)   The length of varchar data type was increased to 65,535 bytes and bit could be used as a data type to manipulate Boolean values in an efficient manner.
(f)   So many optimization improvements were made to speed up queries and data.

### 2.3.5 MySQL 5.1: New Things

MySQL server uses a thread per user and as more and more users connect to the server, its performance reduces but, when MySQL 5.5.16 came up, it had what is called thread pool plugin. This version of MySQL was able to manage number of users with better performance than the previous versions.

MySQL also included MySQL Enterprise Audit. The plugin was designed to meet specification of Oracle. It makes an application to work in consonance with the auditing laws. This is important to both external and internal regulators. A log file is produced to keep record of what the client does in relation to a server such as what tables were accessed, at what time and what were the things executed?

Moreover, this version of MySQL has a default storage engine (InnoDB), which is better than MyISAM. As of  MySQL 5.5.16, it has a provision for using two types of plugins. One is found in MySQL for windows and the other is called PAM (Pluggable Authentication Module). All these are important because the use of native password can now rest and give way to plugins that authenticate users and allow them access to MySQL. These users must not be available in the native grant tables.

MySQL at this stage has decided to move ahead in order to cope with the changing trends in network technology by implementing TCP/IP Connections acceptance of IP version 6. It was a tremendous achievement considering the need for more IP addresses, better connections and better performance.

### 2.3.6 MySQL 5.6: More Functions Added

At this stage, MySQL uses a file called .mylogin.cnf to create authentication documents in an encrypted format through mysql-config-editor. Even when encrypted, it can only be used by a computer's memory. A user cannot see it. This version also has a very powerful encryption system called sha256-password which is better than the previous MD5 password hashing. Sha256_password is stored in a way that, one cannot find the exact password in the database.

The version also had a MySQL password function called validate password strength () that can be used to validate the security of a user's suggested password before acceptance. This need arises because a password that is purely English or common words or names can easily be reveal by brute force attack but, when a password is a mixture of names, numbers and symbols, it is very difficult to attack such users' privacy hence, the issue of password strength .

In addition, indexes using full text can be created and when such indexes are created, the " match () ----- against " statement is used to query. It has been made possible through the use of tables with InnoDB as the database engine.

### 2.4    Web Application Attacks

### 2.4.1 Brief History of Web Application Attacks

In the early days of the commercialisation of the web, attacks were focused on servers and operating systems. As a result of this, software developers started work towards patching these holes against areas of exploit by the attacker. (Watson, 2007). It was after this that attacks were focused on web applications.

According to Information Week (2009), 9 out of ten applications developed for the web had serious security holes. Software from Symantee, Sun, IBM, SAP, Citric and Apache were mostly affected. Moreover, in 2009, over 3,100 flaws were discovered in the first six month of the year. This was said to be 10% more than the ones discovered in the last six months of 2008. InformationWeek (2009) further stressed that in the year 2009, 78% of the flaws were web application type. This was said to be lower than that of 2008 and that 90% of web applications that had security flaws were commercial type while 8% vulnerabilities were found in web browsers. These web applications were said to be capable of exposing sensitive data that belonged to users during transactions. Most of them were cross site and injection type.

InformationWeek (2009) also shaded light on the issue of browser such as Mozilla Firefox, Internet Explorer, Opera and Safari. These popular browsers were said to be vulnerable with Mozilla Firefox being the highest followed by Safari. Though Internet Explorer was lower than Mozilla Firefox and Safari, bugs from Firefox were fixed more quickly than Internet Explorer. Firefox argued this report that, the time it takes to fix a bug was a better factor to consider than the security holes. It further argued that Firefox security system (open security) cannot be compared with Internet Explorer security system (closed system) because they are not similar systems.

In the early days of the web, applications were using a protocol called Common Gateway Interface (CGI), to communicate with the applications that were external. The performance of CGI was not good because it was weak and prone to attacks but as the web became more and more popular, browsers and HTTP came up. Web servers were also available that also allowed developers to produce extensions or plug-ins that allowed more interactions with the server. On the other hand, the development also caused serious problems in form of server exposures to vulnerabilities such as "mod_php multipart form file upload flaw" (Watson, 2007). Watson also stressed that as dot com technology continued to gain popularity, web technology inventions were controlled by functionality and not security. This caused another level of vulnerability to the entire web applications.

## 2.4.2 Some Web Vulnerabilities that have occurred

According to CVE (2013), ext/xml/xml.c that existed in PHP versions lower than 5.3.27 allowed an attacker to remotely cause denial of service (DoS) or other effects that were not crystal clear. Denial of service is a situation where one tries to make a machine or resources that belong to a network inaccessible to users. In this case, the target device is so much saturated with irrelevant requests that it cannot respond to genuine ones. The targets are usually the gateways for card payments and servers that are meant for banks. DoS is a gross violation of the internet policies and illegal in the constitutions of the nations.

Furthermore, "mod_rewrite.c in the mod_rewrite module of the Apache HTTP server 2.2.x before 2.2.25 writes data to a log file without sanitizing non-printable characters, which might allow remote attackers to execute arbitrary commands via an HTTP request containing an escape sequence for a terminal emulator" (CVE, 2013).

CVE (2013) reported that cross-site vulnerabilities were discovered in MiniBB, the version that came before 3.0.1. The file bb_admin.php was very vulnerable because an arbitrary web script could be injected by fraudulent users. This exploit does not need any form of authentication therefore, making this a very subtle attack.

Ragan (2012) said that, PHP vulnerability was by accident made known to the public. The flaws were a code execution flaw. This caused fears due to possibility of attacks on vulnerable websites on a large scale by the attackers. The flaw was said to have been in existence since 2004 but could not be discovered until recently. While the group that first created awareness of this flaw (Eindbazen) were waiting for a patch before the release of the bug, details of the bug were made known to Reddit. This led to the disclosure of what Eindbazen discovered (Ragan, 2012). As a result of this, the development group of PHP encouraged users to upgrade to PHP 5.4.3 as a remedy.

Insertion of data by an application into buffer ought to be done in such a way that there is no overflow. For this to be achieved, the application must check the size of the buffer before insertion of data. If an application fails to do this, it will insert large data that an available buffer cannot take. This often leads to buffer overflow. This was the case of "Eeye June 1999 IIS 4.0 Hack" vulnerability (Security TechCenter, 1999).

When inputs are not properly sanitized and validated, an attacker could gain access to confidential parts of a database. This could later result to greater exposure of users' data and could result to serious problems if not properly checked. The case of "MDAC RDS vulnerability" that affected IIS 4.0 in the month of July, 1999 is a good example (Security TechCenter, 1999). The MDAC (Microsoft Data Access Component) of the server was vulnerable because it could allow illegal user to gain access to a site hosted by the server.

## 2.5   PHP: The Right Ways

OWASP (2013) in her security tip titled "PHP Security Cheat Sheet" gives vital information concerning PHP security. With PHP being the most popular open source scripting language. There is great need to pay attention to the right way of developing PHP applications. The core PHP is considerably safe but other components such as plugins and libraries are not secure, hence the need for proper coding.

## 2.5.1    Injection

OWASP (2013) in her top ten project said that injection is a situation where system especially at the user side send data that cannot be trusted to an interpreter. Vulnerabilities in form of injection are from queries, commands from operating systems and XML parsers. Security holes related to injections are not easy to discover through testing but by close examination of the code. Security holes of this nature are exploited by the attackers through the use of fuzzers and scanners.

Injection can cause serious loss to an organisation through data corruption or access denial. One of the greatest offences you could commit is to deny a legal user access to his/her information. In some situation, the whole data could be stolen and the affected organization left in stranded.

Below is an example of how one could prevent both XSS and SQL injection attacks using PHP.

```
" <?php
    function mysql_entities_fix_string($string)
    {
        return htmlentities(mysql_fix_string($string));
    }
    function mysql_fix_string($string)
    {
            if(get_magic_quotes_gpc())$string= stripslashes($string);
            return mysql_real_escape_string($string);
    }
?> " (Nixon, 2012)
```

One could also access MySQL and stop attacks from XSS as follows:

```
"<?php
    $user  = mysql_entities_fix_string($_POST['user']);
    $pass  = mysql_entities_fix_string($_POST['pass']);
    $query = "SELECT * FROM users WHERE user='$user' AND pass='$pass'";
    function mysql_entities_fix_string($string)
    {
            return htmlentities(mysql_fix_string($string));
    }
    function mysql_fix_string($string)
    {
            if(get_magic_quotes_gpc())$string= stripslashes($string);
```

```
            return mysql_real_escape_string($string);

      }
?>"  (Nixon, 2012).
```

## 2.5.2    Storing Password

Storing passwords as clear text could be very dangerous. This is because confidentiality of your data may be compromised in a situation where a hacker is able to gain access to your site. To take care of this problem, so many password hashing algorithms exist that could be used to prevent unwanted users from gaining access to the database. This can be achieved through the use of functions such as MD5, sha256, Crypt and Bcrypt functions.

All these functions convert password to random strings longer the real plaintext and they are usually stored in databases by developers. The stored password is irreversible. For a statement such as "md5 ('mypassword')" (Nixon, 2012), converts password into 32 numbers that are hexadecimal . The sha256, crypt and Bcrypt are said to be better than md5 algorithm.

Some of these password hashing algorithms could be subjected to brute force attack by some other software that one could get from the internet. To solve this problem, there exists a technique called "salting" where the real password is surrounded with some other strings before hashing then database storage. It is not easy with this technique to use a particular software and decrypt the password.

## 2.5.3 PHP: Upgrading

OWASP's Security Cheat Sheet (2013) advices that people should develop the habit of upgrading to higher and stable version since support for such versions are always available. OWASP (2013) further stressed that there is currently no support for PHP 5.2.x. Developers are advised to upgrade to version 5.4.x or 5.3.x. As a result of this, any website that is powered by PHP 5.2.x may have some vulnerability. Operational servers are the most recommended for upgrading PHP because attacker use the known vulnerabilities and attack servers at random. Use latest and stable PHP (5.5). For new developer or new into PHP development world, the best advice is to start development with any version that is the latest and stable. This is because most of the stable versions did not come to be overnight. It was through series of developments by the PHP team and the contributions of several organisations and individuals that results to a stable version. Such versions must have passed through several patches or changes before a stable version is released. The current stable version is PHP 5.5 (Lockhart, Jordan, Sturgeon, 2013). The version differences in terms of numbers such as PHP 5.5 and PHP 5.2 signifies major differences or adjustments that are believed to have made the higher version better. PHP.net could be used as a reference point for latest information about functions and constructs.

### 2.5.4 UTF-8 Character Set

UTF-8 is a very popular character encoding used on the Internet today. E-mail programs are also expected to create and open mails using UTF-8. The character encoding has gained popularity in programming and operating systems. The importance of using UTF-8 character set cannot be overemphasized considering its proven reliability amongst the developers of the World Wide Web. So, UTF-8 character encoding is highly recommended during database creation and front end development.

### 2.5.5 Standard Ways of Writing Codes

According to PHP the Right Way (2013), the PHP community is made up of so many libraries, components and frameworks. As a result of this, the need for setting standards of writing codes arises. This results to conformity and other developers can easily understand such codes. There are standards such as PSR-0 , PSR_1 and PSR-2, Zend coding and PEAR coding standards. These standards are meant for individuals and groups that belong to a particular framework or library to follow.

To check against these recommendations is not an easy task. There exists software such as PHP Codessniffer that can be used to check if codes written by a developer conforms to the laid down rules of the standard. However, for one to find relief from the tediousness of following standards, PHP Coding Standard Fixer could be used to modify code syntax so that it works in consonance with the laid down guides. It saves the time used to debug by hand.

### 2.5.6 PHP Namespaces

PHP The Right Way (2013) gave insight into namespaces. It can be compared with directories in an operating system. PHP has a community of developers from various areas developing libraries. These libraries contain classes that may have the same names and when brought together could result to confusion. This confusion has been resolved by the PHP community using

19

the idea of developing classes that may have the same names but within a separate namespace. This is highly recommended by coding standards such as PSR-0.

## 2.6` Keeping the Software Secure

Kameshwaran (2012), in a book titled "Software Testing" said that keeping the software secure means to hinder from inappropriate or abnormal use of the system. Security is an issue that affects every software system. Sometimes people take software security for granted, forgetting the fact that, no amount of money judiciously spent on security is too much, considering the devastating effects of insecure system.

Kameshwaran further expatiated that, OWASP's recommendation for what a team of security experts are to check for during security testing are:

- "Account Lockout Attack
- Argument Injection or Modification
- Asymmetric Resource Consumption (Amplification)
- Binary Planting Blind SQL Injection
- Blind Xpath Injection
- Brute Force Attack
- Buffer Overflow Attack
- Cache Poisoning
- Cash Overflow
- Code Injection
- Command Injection
- Comment Injection Attack
- Cross Frame Scriptin
- Cross Site History Manipulation (XSHM)
- Cross Site Tracing
- Cross Site Request Forgery (CSRF)
- Cross-site Scripting
- Cross-user Defacement
- Cryptanalysis
- Custom Special Character Injection
- Denial of Service
- Direct Dynamic Code Evaluation (Eval Injection)
- Direct Static Code Injection

- Double Encoding, Force Browsing
- Format String Attack
- Full Path Disclosure
- HTTP Request Smuggling
- HTTP Response Splitting
- LDAP Injection
- Man-in-the-browser Attack
- Man-in-the-middle Attack
- Mobile Code: Invoking Un-trust Mobile Code
- Mobile Code: Non-final Public Field
- Mobile Mode: Object Hijack
- Network Eavesdropping
- One-click Attack
- Overflow Binary Resource File
- Page Hijacking
- Parameter Delimiter
- Path Manipulation
- Regular Expression Denial of Service
- Relative Path Traversal
- Server-side Includes (SSI) Injection
- Session Hijacking Attack
- Session Prediction
- Special Element Injection
- Spyware, SQL Injection
- Trojan Horse
- Unicode Encoding.
- Web Parameter Tampering " (Kameshwaran, 2012)

But this long list of what to check for is said to have some that are irrelevant. As a result of this, Kameshwaran (2012) said that, any testing team is advised to consider if the software system is not able to achieve any of the following qualities:

(a) Availability: The testing team should ensure that the services and the information expected from the system are provided when needed.
(b) Non-repudiation: There should be a mechanism to ensure that if someone sent something through the system, that person cannot deny his/her action.

(c) Confidentiality: Information must be well protected especially the confidential ones. Users that have no access right must not be allowed to have access to information. This is one of the most sensitive aspects of system security. Things like bank account information or details of an individual in a country's databank must be protected by the system.

(d) Integrity: The system should have a mechanism whereby the user approves that information given is as expected one and has no mistake(s).

(e) Authentication: The system should confirm if a user is a genuine user of that system.

(f) Authorisation: If (e) above is true then the next level is to determine if the user is allowed to have access to the entire system or some parts of the system. Imagine a fraudulent user who tries to have access to somebody's bank account or somebody who tries to intrude into people's privacy by accessing details of individuals in the database and so on. Testing team must check against this menace.

# 3     Chapter 3      Secure PHP Project Execution

## 3.1   Introduction

Here, the authors want to start with a problem and then shed light on how to solve such problem in an acceptable manner: What must we do in order to develop a secure application/admission portal for a tertiary institution? How do we go about this? We are going to start with areas that are important but don't have much security implications then go into the secure part of this project. Every site developed using PHP is supposed to follow request/response sequence of the client/server (Nixon,2012). Figure 3.1 shows this.

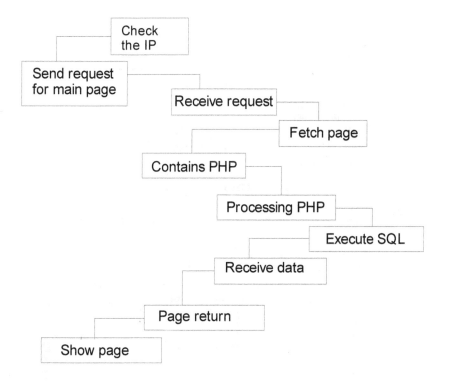

Figure 3.1 Request/response sequence of the client/server
Source: Robin Nixon (2012) PHP, MySQL, JavaScript & CSS

Now, let us assume that we are going to develop a web portal for a tertiary institution and the name of the institution is called InstitutionA with two faculties: FacultyA and FacultyB. Some steps must be followed to minimize mistakes, though they may be repeated severally in form of a circle before a final and acceptable application is developed.

## 3.2 Get an Estimated Time for Completion of the Project

If you have an estimate of when to start and when to complete then, you can prepare a time table such as table 3.1 below.

| Activity | Time of Start | Time to Stop | Days |
|---|---|---|---|
| Get the required functionality of the new system | 01/06/2013 | 05/06/2013 | 5 |
| Update your knowledge of some of the following: *PHP *MySQL *HTML *JavaScript *CSS *Jquery | 06/06/2013 | 10/06/2013 | 5 |
| Produce an architectural design of the new system | 11/06/2013 | 16/06/2013 | 6 |
| Database and Front End Design | 17/06/2013 | 20/06/2013 | 4 |
| Coding | 21/06/2013 | 1/07/2013 | 11 |
| Testing | 02/07/2013 | 03/07/2013 | 2 |

Table 3.1 Proposed time for project activities

## 3.3 Get the Required Functionality of the System

Go to the organization that wants you to develop the web portal and document all details from them but know that you are an expert so you can also make valuable recommendations to them on areas that need amendments. Don't claim to be a jack of all trades because you may be a master of none. The organization is the user so you must be conscious of this throughout the period of the web portal development.

## 3.4 Update Your Knowledge

If you continue to develop applications with your previous knowledge and refuse to research on recent inventions, available updates and innovations then, your work will soon become obsolete. A good web developer is also a good researcher.

## 3.5  Design the Architecture of the Site You Want to Develop

In this case, InstitutionA is used as an example. InstitutionA website ought to be developed in such a way that applicants could access some parts of the website through the homepage. Based on the principle of authorisation, authentication, integrity, confidentiality and availability, students that applied for admission are expected to check their statuses through their suggested passwords and usernames. The password and usernames is supposed to be stored in the database during online application for admission.

Applicants are expected to see either the entire admission list or faculty admission list, based on what the school needs. Individuals could also see their application statuses. The management of the institution will be given admin password and admin username. The admin right given by the software developer, empowers the institution to give admission(s) to qualified candidate(s). Figure 3.2 below shows the design. The design shows how various functionality link to one another. By doing this, your coding will be with great focus.

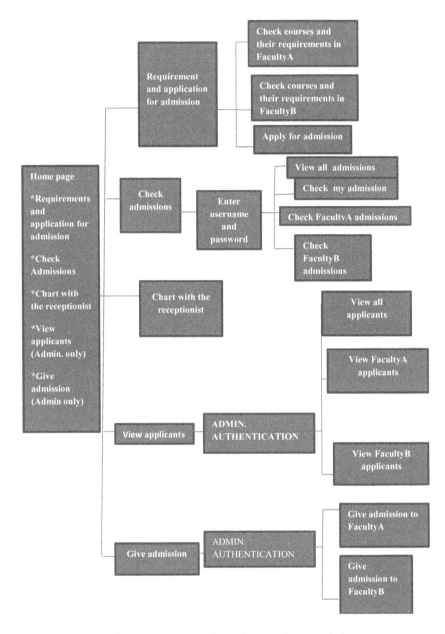

Figure 3.2 The design of InstitutionA website

## 3.6    Database and Front End Design of InstititionA

What you need to do here is to think, draw the database tables and label them, bearing in mind the PHP codes and the sql queries that could give the functionalities that were recommended by the management of the institution. Remember we told you not to forget what the user wants. This should be done before you think of the sql commands that will produce the desired database and its tables. The following questions may be important based on the requirement:

a    How does one check the list of all admitted student of InstitutionA for a particular year?

b    How do we see the list of those admitted into FacultyA?

c    How does one see the list of those admitted  into FacultyB?

d    How can the management see the list of all applicants?

e    What query will enable the view of all those that applied for admission into  into FacultyA?

f    What query will enable the view of all those that applied for admission into  into FacultyB?

g    What query will allow the management only to give admission into FacultyA?

h    What query will allow the management only to give admission into FacultyB?

i    What query will be used to record inputs  from application form into the database?

Based on the questions above, you may consider creating two tables: Details table (table 3.2) and Academic table (table 3.3). ApplicantId column of table 3.2 is a primary key but becomes a foreign key in table 3.3. Answers to the following questions will not be a database function since ordinary html link could do so:

a    How do users communicate with InstitutionA receptionist through Facebook?

b    How do users check the requirement for admissions into all the departments in FacultyA and FacultyB?

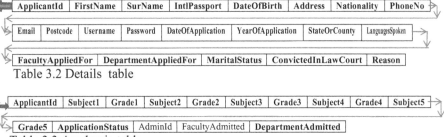

| ApplicantId | FirstName | SurName | IntlPassport | DateOfBirth | Address | Nationality | PhoneNo |
|---|---|---|---|---|---|---|---|
| Email | Postcode | Username | Password | DateOfApplication | YearOfApplication | StateOrCounty | LanguagesSpoken |
| FacultyAppliedFor | DepartmentAppliedFor | MaritalStatus | ConvictedInLawCourt | Reason | | | |

Table 3.2 Details table

| ApplicantId | Subject1 | Grade1 | Subject2 | Grade2 | Subject3 | Grade3 | Subject4 | Grade4 | Subject5 |
|---|---|---|---|---|---|---|---|---|---|
| Grade5 | ApplicationStatus | AdminId | FacultyAdmitted | DepartmentAdmitted | | | | | |

Table 3.3 Academic table

You may decide to use one table in the database but this type of design is not encouraged for large databases, see Table 3.4 below.

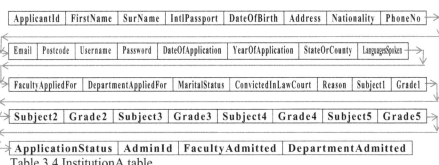

| ApplicantId | FirstName | SurName | IntlPassport | DateOfBirth | Address | Nationality | PhoneNo |
|---|---|---|---|---|---|---|---|
| Email | Postcode | Username | Password | DateOfApplication | YearOfApplication | StateOrCounty | LanguagesSpoken |
| FacultyAppliedFor | DepartmentAppliedFor | MaritalStatus | ConvictedInLawCourt | Reason | Subject1 | Grade1 | |
| Subject2 | Grade2 | Subject3 | Grade3 | Subject4 | Grade4 | Subject5 | Grade5 |
| ApplicationStatus | AdminId | FacultyAdmitted | DepartmentAdmitted | | | | |

Table 3.4 InstitutionA table

Also draw your front end pages before you write codes that could produce what you drew. This will make your work easier, and you should always bear in mind that your forms at the front end are related to the table(s) at the back end. This will save you from the headache of redesign. Imagine that you want to develop a simple home page like Figure 3.3 or a form like Figure 3.4 then, you need to draw it before coding. It may not look nice like that of an artist but by drawing it, you are like a traveller that knows his/her destination.

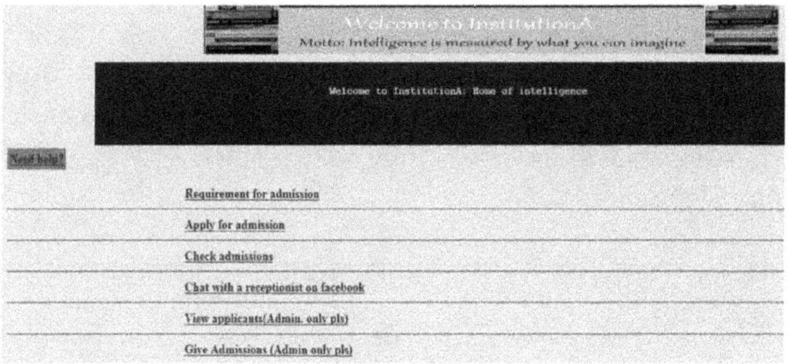
Welcome to InstitutionA
Motto: Intelligence is measured by what you can imagine
Welcome to InstitutionA: Home of intelligence
Need help?
Requirement for admission
Apply for admission
Check admissions
Chat with a receptionist on facebook
View applicants(Admin. only pls)
Give Admissions (Admin only pls)

Figure3.3: A simple home page

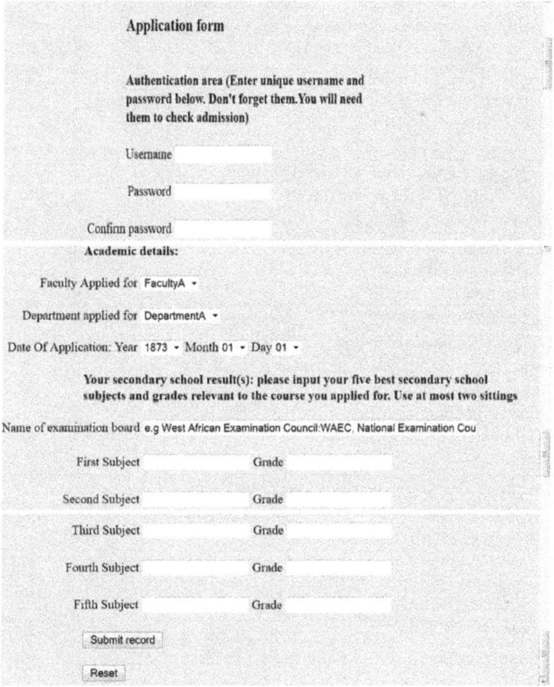
Application form
Authentication area (Enter unique username and password below. Don't forget them.You will need them to check admission)
Username
Password
Confirm password
Academic details:
Faculty Applied for FacultyA
Department applied for DepartmentA
Date Of Application: Year 1873 Month 01 Day 01
Your secondary school result(s): please input your five best secondary school subjects and grades relevant to the course you applied for. Use at most two sittings
Name of examination board e.g West African Examination Council:WAEC, National Examination Cou
First Subject Grade
Second Subject Grade
Third Subject Grade
Fourth Subject Grade
Fifth Subject Grade
Submit record
Reset

Figure 3.4: Form

## 3.7 Coding

Coding is a very important part of web development but, it is a very good practice to employ the services of a security expert. Develop your personal test plan, write your codes and then use the test plan to test your software before handing it over to a security expert. Now, using institutionA as earlier mentioned , a test plan for InstitutionA site ought to be developed and the web developer is expected to write codes in such a way that when tested as recommended by the test plan, it should not be found wanting. More explanations on this will be given in the next chapter. Table 3.5 is the test plan. The last two columns will be filled in the next chapter. That is, usually done during testing of the site.

| Test No | Description | Test Data | Expected Result | Pass/Fail | Comments |
|---|---|---|---|---|---|
| 1 | Superglobals at the back end | Check for the use of SQL and XSS injection attack-prevention code | SQL and XSS injection attack-prevention code was used | | |
| 2 | Malicious code that can make an attacker to have access to the database without admin right | Inject username with malicious code such as (daniel1'"';#), leave the password field empty and click ok or sent | The database should deny access to this attacker | | |
| 3 | Send a malicious code that could delete all data in the database | Use malicious code (anything' OR 1=1 #) for username field but leave password field empty and click ok or send | Nothing was deleted from the database as a result of this action | | |
| 4 | Login file that will be used to Connect to database | Check for the use of require_once to indirectly send the host name, database name, username and password during database connection | The page was able to connect to database through the use of require_once. | | |
| 5 | User can send inputs to the database using Get or Post but Post is preferred | Check to see if all users' inputs were sent by post or Get | All input sent from the front end were by post | | |
| 6 | MySQLi or PDO is better than MySQL connect during database connection | MySQLi or PDO connections | All connections to database were done with either MySQLi or PDO keywords | | |
| 7 | Password hashing through the use of crypt or Bcrypt | Check all areas that require password for access to database | All the passwords were hashed using Crypt or Bcrypt | | |
| 8 | Textbox's hidden field | Check all the textboxes that are meant for password at the back end | All password fields don't show clear text | | |
| 9 | Use of InnoDB | Check the database | The database uses | | |

30

| | | | | | |
|---|---|---|---|---|---|
| | and UTF-8 character encoding | and the front end for the use of UTF-8 character encoding and InnoDB as the engine. | InnoDB as the database engine and UTF-8 was chosen for character encoding at both back end and front end | | |
| 10 | Navigation from one page to another | Check navigation links within the website | One could use the navigation links provided on the site to move from one page to another without necessarily depending on the browser's navigation | | |
| 11 | Application for admission | All fields should be filled with inputs | • Report successful submission<br>• Show a logout link or homepage | | |
| 12 | Application for admission | Some important fields such as name, email, o level grade, username and password should not be filled | * The System should remind you to fill all the fields that are compulsory if you refused or forgot to fill all but clicked send.<br>* The system should link you back to previous page for amendment. | | |
| 13 | Check application status | If an applicant applied for admission, the applicant should be able to check his/her application status by doing the following:<br>• Click Check Admissions link then<br>• Click check my admission link<br>Then type correct username and password such as leku1 for username and leku2 for password-all small letters. | The applicant should be shown his/her status as follows:<br>• Your application is being processed or<br>• You were not admitted or<br>• If you were admitted, your admission letter should be shown to you | | |
| 14 | Check | Input password and | Message such as | | |

| | | username that are wrong or make one of them to be wrong as follows:<br><br>• Click Check Admissions link then<br>• Click check my admission link<br><br>Then type wrong username and password or one of them wrong such as master1 for username and master2 for password | wrong Username/password should be displayed and a link to previous page and home page (logout) should be provided. | | |
|---|---|---|---|---|---|
| | application status | | | | |
| 15 | View applicants or give admission | Enter correct admin username and password Such as daniel1 for username and daniel2 for password. | Allow admin to view applications and also give admissions to students. | | |
| 16 | View applicants or give admission | Enter wrong admin username and password | Deny access to giving of admission or view of applicants' list | | |
| 17 | Chart with a receptionist | Click chart with receptionist and type your Facebook address and send | The receptionist is able to accept your request using different machine and charting starts | | |

Figure 3.5: Test Plan of the System

# 4 Chapter 4 System Testing, Discussion and Analysis of Result

Assuming that InstitutionA web portal has been developed then, what next? The next thing to do before you invite any reputable security expert to also look at it is to implement what is in the test plan and fill the last two columns of the test plan. Please, have a look at table 4.6 below.

| Test No | Description | Test Data | Expected Result | Pass/Fail | Comments |
|---|---|---|---|---|---|
| 1 | Superglobals at the back end | Check for the use of SQL and XSS injection attack-prevention code | SQL and XSS injection attack-prevention code was used | Pass | User inputs were encoded and that prevents injection |
| 2 | Malicious code that can make an attacker to have access to the database without admin right | Inject username with malicious code such as (daniel1'";#), leave the password field empty and click ok or sent | The database should deny access to this attacker | Pass | Even if there is a user with username called daniel1, the # used cannot penetrate the site. |
| 3 | Send a malicious code that could delete all data in the database | Use malicious code (anything' OR 1=1 #) for username field but leave password field empty and click ok or send | Nothing was deleted from the database as a result of this action | | There was no provision for deleting data from the database in the developed site so, this malicious code is not applicable |
| 4 | Login file that will be used to Connect to database | Check for the use of require_once to indirectly send the host name, database name, username and password during database connection | The page was able to connect to database through the use of require_once. | Pass | Require_once was used for all database access. |
| 5 | User can send inputs to the database using Get or Post but Post is preferred | Check to see if all users' inputs were sent by post or Get | All input sent from the front end were by post | Pass | Post was used throughout |
| 6 | MySQLi or PDO is better | MySQLi or PDO connections | All connections to database were done | Pass | Mysqli was used in all |

| | | | | | |
|---|---|---|---|---|---|
| | than MySQL connect during database connection | | with either MySQLi or PDO keywords | | database connections |
| 7 | Password hashing through the use of crypt or Bcrypt | Check all areas that require password for access to database | All the passwords were hashed using Crypt or Bcrypt | Pass | Crypt was used for all password hashing. |
| 8 | Textbox's hidden field | Check all the textboxes that are meant for password at the back end | All password fields don't show clear text | Pass | Passwords were not shown in clear text |
| 9 | Use of InnoDB and UTF-8 character encoding | Check the database and the front end for the use of UTF-8 character encoding and InnoDB as the engine. | The database uses InnoDB as the database engine and UTF-8 was chosen for character encoding at both back end and front end | Pass | Based on the database structure, InnoDB was used as database engine and UTF-8 was used for character encoding |
| 10 | Navigation from one page to another | Check navigation links within the website | One could use the navigation links provided on the site to move from one page to another without necessarily depending on the browser's navigation | Pass | Hyperlinks were used |
| 11 | Application for admission | All fields should be filled with inputs | • Report successful submission<br>• Show a logout link or homepage | Pass | Shows result as expected |
| 12 | Application for admission | Some important fields such as name, email, o level grade, username and password should not be filled | * The System should remind you to fill all the fields that are compulsory if you refused or forgot to fill all but clicked send.<br>* The system should link you back to previous page for amendment. | pass | If one refuses to fill some important fields and clicks enter, a general statement such as you must fill all the fields except ....was used and a link |

| | | | | | provided for amendment |
|---|---|---|---|---|---|
| 13 | Check application status | If an applicant applied for admission, the applicant should be able to check his/her application status by doing the following: <br> • Click Check Admissions link then <br> • Click check my admission link <br> Then type correct username and password such as leku1 for username and leku2 for password-all in small letters. | The applicant should be shown his/her status as follows: <br> • Your application is being processed or <br> • You were not admitted or <br> • If you were admitted, your admission letter should be shown to you | Pass | Works as expected |
| 14 | Check application status | Input password and username that are wrong or make one of them to be wrong as follows: <br> • Click Check Admissions link then <br> • Click check my admission link <br> Then type wrong username and password or one of them wrong such as master1 for username and master2 for password | Message such as wrong Username/password should be displayed and a link to previous page and home page (logout) should be provided. | Pass | The message was displayed and the links provided |
| 15 | View applicants or give admission | Enter correct admin username and password Such as daniel1 for username and daniel2 for password. | Allow admin to view applications and also give admissions to students. | Pass | The given admin username and password were able to do what they were meant for |
| 16 | View applicants or give admission | Enter wrong admin username and password | Deny access to giving of admission or view of | Pass | The denial was successful |

| | | | applicants' list | | |
|---|---|---|---|---|---|
| 17 | Chart with a receptionist | Click chart with receptionist and type your Facebook address and send | The receptionist is able to accept your request using different machine and charting starts | Pass | Charting is possible if the system is connected to the internet |

Table 4.6 Result of a test conducted on the developed system

Now, the next thing to do is to to expatiate on this test through discussion and analysis of the system with pictorial evidences. This will give better understanding of what the test plan tries to achieve.

## 4.1  A Malicious Code (daniel1'";#)

A form like figure 4.3 may be developed   for authentication in InstitutionA web portal but, if there exists a username  in the database called daniel1, which is easy to guess in a large organization, then, it could be injected at the front end by typing **daniel1'";#** as the username. If you leave the password field empty and click ok (Figure 4.3). This malicious code will surely cause your PHP code and your SQL command to allow access to your confidential data if proper codes were not written. This code is best understood with an SQL example:

**Query="select * from InstitutionATable where Username='$username' and password='$password'";**

If **$username=daniel1'";#**  was sent from a textbox at the front end and was accepted by post then, substitute it in the above query, it becomes

**Query="select * from InstitutionATable where Username='daniel1'";#' and password='password'";**   Wau!! The # symbol has rendered the remaining query useless and it therefore becomes malicious. The malicious query now looks like this:

**Query="select * from InstitutionATable where Username='daniel1'";** .
This renders the password irrelevant but a web developer must be smart by writing PHP codes that prevent this. You can overcome this problem in the following ways:

a) Use a logical PHP codes that forces a user to input both username and password before any query is sent to the database. See Figure 4.1

36

```
if (!$Username || !$Password1)
{
    echo '<br /><table bgcolor="Antiquewhite" border="1">
    <tr><td><p><a href="../index.php">Previous page</a></p></td>

    <td><p><a href="../../index.php">logout</a></p></td></tr></table><br /><br />';
    echo "Please fill all the fields before you proceed<br />";

    return;
```

Figure 4.1: PHP code that forces a user to input both username and password before any query is sent to the database.

a)      Use injection prevention code. See Figure 4.2

```
11    $Username=$db->real_escape_string(htmlspecialchars($Username));
12    $Password1=$db->real_escape_string(htmlspecialchars($Password1));
```

Figure 4.2: Injection prevention code

Figures 4.3 shows the website being injected with malicious admin Username.

Figure 4.3 Injection attempt with admin username

See Figure 4.4, it shows how the web portal handles the malicious code.

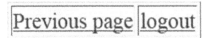

Previous page |logout

Please fill all the fields before you proceed

Figure 4.4: Message that comes out when a malicious code is injected

## 4.2 Use of 'Require_once' for Access to Login Page and the use of mysqli for Connection to Database

Use 'require_once' for access to login page of the database and also use mysqli for connection to the database. These are regarded as good programming practices. Check and make sure that all your codes were written in that style of coding. See Figure 4.5 Also see Figure 4.6 for how a login page should be specially developed. Alternatively, you could also use PDO for your database connection.

```php
<?php
    require_once 'login.php';
    @ $db = new mysqli("$db_localhost","$db_username","$db_password","$db_database");
    if(mysqli_Connect_errno()){
        echo 'Error: Could not connect to database';
        exit;
    }
```

Figure 4.5: login using require_once and mysqli connection to database

```php
<?php // login.php
    $db_hostname = 'localhost';
    $db_database = 'InstitutionA';
    $db_username = 'leku';
    $db_password = 'lekuleku';
?>
```

Figure 4.6: PHP login page

## 4.3 InnoDB Database Engine and UTF-8 Character Encoding

Figure4.7 is part of the InstitutionA database gotten from phpmyadmin. If you export this database and open it with a text editor such as Editra or Notepad++, you will see the database engine and the character encoding used.

Use any database engine that can handle transaction such as InnoDB for your web portal. Both figure 4.7 and figure 4.8 show that the character encoding was UTF-8. This shows that, the database is able to handle transactions effectively because of the database engine used. The character encoding is one of the most popular being used on the Internet due to its proven reliability. You should also use utf8 at the front end based on HTML5 to help the browser determine how to render the content. See Figure 4.9. They all contribute to the security of a system.

```
113    KEY  Grades_2  ( Grades (20)),
114    KEY `Grade5_3` (`Grade5`(20)),
115    KEY `ApplicationStatus` (`ApplicationStatus`(20)),
116    KEY `AdminId` (`AdminId`),
117    KEY `FacultyAdmitted` (`FacultyAdmitted`(20)),
118    KEY `FacultyAdmitted_2` (`FacultyAdmitted`(20)),
119    KEY `DepartmentAdmitted` (`DepartmentAdmitted`(20)),
120    KEY `YearOfApplication` (`YearOfApplication`)
121  ) ENGINE=InnoDB DEFAULT CHARSET=utf8 AUTO_INCREMENT=17 ;
122
```

Figure 4.7: The database (Institutiona), exported and opened using a text editor (Editra)

| # | Name | Type | Collation | Attributes | Null | Default | Extra |
|---|------|------|-----------|------------|------|---------|-------|
| 1 | Applicantid | int(10) | | UNSIGNED | No | None | AUTO_INCREMI |
| 2 | Username | varchar(100) | utf8_general_ci | | Yes | NULL | |
| 3 | Password | varchar(100) | utf8_general_ci | | Yes | NULL | |
| 4 | FirstName | varchar(100) | utf8_general_ci | | Yes | NULL | |
| 5 | MiddleName | varchar(100) | utf8_general_ci | | Yes | NULL | |
| 6 | Surname | varchar(100) | utf8_general_ci | | Yes | NULL | |
| 7 | IntlPassport | varchar(100) | utf8_general_ci | | Yes | NULL | |
| 8 | DateOfBirth | int(10) | | UNSIGNED | Yes | NULL | |
| 9 | Address | varchar(100) | utf8_general_ci | | Yes | NULL | |
| 10 | Nationality | varchar(100) | utf8_general_ci | | Yes | NULL | |
| 11 | PhoneNo | varchar(100) | utf8_general_ci | | Yes | NULL | |
| 12 | StateOrCounty | varchar(100) | utf8_general_ci | | Yes | NULL | |

Figure 4.8: Database structure of some columns of InstitutionA database, using phpmyadmin.

```
<!DOCTYPE html>

<html>

<head>

<link rel="stylesheet" type="text/css" href="./././All/background.css" />

<meta charset = "utf-8">

</head>

</body>

</body>

</html>
```

Figure 4.9: utf8 at the front end

## 4.4 Use of Crypt Password Hashing with Salt

Use Crypt password hashing or any reliable one for storing passwords in the database (InstitutionA database). Also use salting to make passwords more secured. This is a secure coding practice that is highly recommended and encouraged by PHP web developers. See Figure 4.10 below.

```
27      $Password="$Password1";
28      $salt2="5555555555555555666666666wwwtthbhhnn";
29      $encrpt=crypt($Password,$salt2);
```

Figure 4.10: Use of crypt and salt for inputs and output authentication

## 4.5 Access to the Web Portal

In the case of InstitutionA, the admin is allowed to access almost every part of the portal but students have some restrictions. Links like requirements for admission, apply for admission, view of entire admission list is possible for all users. See Figure 4.11 and Figure 4.12.

However, links like check my admission (Figure 4.12) is confidential so the applicant must type correct username and password (Figure 4.13) before such applicant is allowed to see his/her status and the status is one of the three possibilities (admitted or being processed or not admitted) and if a candidate is admitted. The candidate is allowed to see an admission letter online. If not, appropriate message is displayed. This is assumed to be in consonance with what that institution wants. So, yours may not be like this but know that there are different levels of access in a web portal.

40

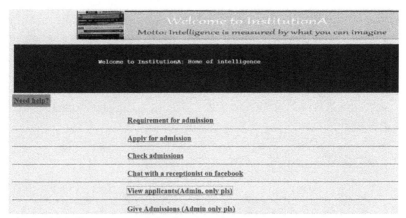

Figure 4.11: Home page of the developed system

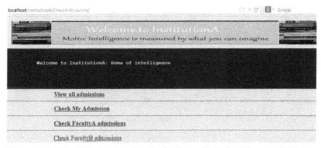

Figure 4.12 : Click check admissions link in Figure 4.11 to see this

Figure 4.13: Restricting access to confidential part of a document

Also, links that have relationship with view of all applicants and giving of admissions are under the total control of the admin. So, no applicant's

41

username and password can do this except the unique username and password (daniel1 and daniel2 respectively) together with a unique AdminID of one (1) provided in the database for the admin. Every other applicant has an adminID of two (2) which restrict them from viewing official pages. Check AdmintId column of the affected part of institutiona database below (Figure 4.14). The Id (2) was assigned to the database as a constant for every applicant using PHP while the Id (1) meant for admin was assigned using phpmyadmin since only few admin Ids are required in an organization.

Figure 4.14: part of Institutiona database showing admin id of 1 for admin. and 2 for all other applicants, viewed using phpmyadmin.

This depends on how you think. What is done here was to develop another column called Adminid in the database table such that, apart from checking your username and password, the query/PHP code will go further to know your Adminid. If it is 2 then, you are an applicant; you are restricted from having access to confidential part of the site. But if it is 1 then, you can access almost all parts of the site. You may say 1 and 2 are easy to guess but I want to ask you, how were they inserted in the database? The code was written in such a way that, anytime somebody applied, an Adminid of 2 is automatically stored in the database but for the management, the Adminid of 1 was stored using different method. Since the passwords for the management of an institution are usually few, the authors sent the usernames and the encrypted passwords from the front end and then manually changed the Adminid in the database using phpmyadmin. Remember, the usernames and passwords give access to users but it is the Adminid that determines a user's level of access. This situation always arises when access to a web portal are in levels

## 4.6    No File Extension

Name every web page as index so that when they are loaded, the names of the pages that were loaded will not show. This means the file extensions will not also show and this implies that no attacker will understand the technology used in developing your website. You need to create your links to folders and not files, to be able to achieve this. This method also contributes to the security of a site.

Another method is to use .htaccess file to hinder a web page from showing its name and its file extension. See Figure 4.15 If you save this file with a file name .htaccess using Notepad++ or any text editor in the same folder with a web page called index.php then, anytime you link to the folder, index.php will be loaded but the browser will not show the file name or the file extension.

```
<IfModule mod_rewrite.c>

    RewriteEngine on

    RewriteCond %{REQUEST_FILENAME}    !-d

    RewriteCond %{REQUEST_FILENAME}    !-f

    RewriteRule .                      ./index.php [L]

</IfModule>
```

Figure 4.15: .htaccess file

## References

Addison Wesley Longman, (1998). A History of HTML [online] Available at < http://www.w3.org/people/Ragget/book4/ch02.html > [Accessed 25 August 2013]

BusinessDictionary.com (2013). Model [online] Available at < **http://www.businessdictionary.com/definition/model.html > [Accessed 2nd August 2013]**

CERT, (2009). CERT Statistics (Historical)[online] Available at< http://www.cert.org/stats/cert_stats.html/ > [Accessed 21st June, 2013] > [Accessed 21st June, 2013]

CVE, (2013). Common Vulnerabilities and Exposures [online] Available at < http://cve.mitre.org/cgi-bin/cvename.cgi?name=cve-2013-4113 > [Accessed 11 July 2013]

CVE, (2013). CVE-2013-1862 [online] Available at <

http://cve.mitre.org/cgi-bin/cvename.cgi?name=cve-2013-1862 > [Accessed 12 July 2013]


CVE, (2013). CVE-2013-5020 [online] Available at <
http://cve.mitre.org/cgi-bin/cvename.cgi?name=cve-2013-5020 > [Accessed 13 July 2013]

InformationWeek, (2009). 9 In 10 Web Apps Have Serious Flaws; The 10 most Severe software vulnerabilities during the first half of 2009 affected software from Apache, Citrix, IBM, SAP, Sun, and Symantee, among other organizations Available through: Anglia Ruskin University Library website < http://Libweb.anglia.ac.uk > [Accessed 7 August 2013]

Jovanovic, N., Kruegel, C., and Kirda, E., (2006). Pixy: A Static Analysis Tool for Detecting Web Application Vulnerabilities. Security and Privacy. 2006 IEEE Symposium 6pp-263 Berkeley/Oakland, CA [online] Available at <http://ieeexplore.ieee.org/xpl/login.jsp?tp=&arnumber=1624016&url=http%3A%2F%2Fiee explore.ieee.org%2Fxpls%2Fabs_all.jsp%3Farnumber%3D1624016>[Accessed 8th June, 2013]

Kameshwaran, R., (2012). Software Testing 1st edition Marston Gate: Amazone.co.uk Ltd

Lockhart, J., Jordan, K., and Sturgeon, P., (2013). PHP The Right Way [online] Available at <http://www.phptherightway.com/ > [Accessed 29 June 2013]

Lockhart, J., (2013). PHP The Right Way [online] Available at < http://www.phptherightway.com > [Accessed 5 July 2013]

MySQL, (2013). History of MySQL [online] Available at< http://dev.mysql.com/doc/refman/5.0/en/history.html > [Accessed 5th August, 2013]

MySQL, (2013). What is MySQL? [online] Available at< http://dev.mysql.com/doc/refman/5.0/en/what-is-mysql.html > [Accessed 5th August, 2013]

MySQL, (2013). The Main Features of MySQL [online] Available at< http://dev.mysql.com/doc/refman/5.0/en/features.html > [Accessed 5th August, 2013]

MySQL, (2013). MySQL Development History [online] Available at< http://dev.mysql.com/doc/refman/5.0/en/development-history.html > [Accessed 5th August,2013]

MySQL, (2013). Upgrading MySQL [online] Available at< http://dev.mysql.com/doc/refman/5.0/en/upgrading.html > [Accessed 5th August, 2013]

MySQL, (2013). What is New in MySQL 5.0 [online] Available at<

http://dev.mysql.com/doc/refman/5.0/mysql-nutshell.html > [Accessed 5th August, 2013]

MySQL, (2013). What is New in MySQL 5.1 [online] Available at<
http://dev.mysql.com/doc/refman/5.1/en/mysql-nutshell.html > [Accessed 5th August, 2013]

MySQL, (2013). What is New in MySQL 5.5 [online] Available at<
http://dev.mysql.com/doc/refman/5.5/en/mysql-nutshell.html > [Accessed 5th August, 2013]

MySQL, (2013). What is New in MySQL 5.6 [online] Available at<
http://dev.mysql.com/doc/refman/5.6/en/mysql-nutshell.html > [Accessed 5th August, 2013]

Nixon, R., (2012). PHP, MySQL, JavaScript & CSS. Sebastopol: O'Reilly, Inc.

OIS, (2004). Guidelines for Security Vulnerability and Response: Organization for

OWASP, (2013). PHP Security Cheat Sheet. [online] Available at<
https://www.owasp.org/index.php/php_Security_Cheat_Sheet > [Accessed 12 July, 2013]

PHP, (2013). History of PHP [online] Available at<
http://php.net/manual/en/hostory.php >[Accessed 5th August, 2013]

Ragan, S., (2012). Official Fix for PHP Flaw Easily Bypassed, Researchers say, Security Week [online] Available at
<http://www.securityweek.com/official-fix-php-flaw-easily-
bypassed-researchers-say > [Accessed 1 July 2013]

Security TechCenter, (1999). Patch Available for "malformed HTR request" vulnerability: Microsoft Security Bulletin ms99-019 [online] Available at <
http://technet.microsoft.com/en-us/security/bulletin/ms99-019 >[Accessed 23 June 2013]

Watson, D., (2007). Web Application Attacks: Network Security volume 2007 Issue 10 Available through Anglia Ruskin University < http://Libweb.anglia.ac.uk >
[Accessed 15 August 2013]

W3C, (2013). What is CSS? [online] Available at < http://www.w3.org/style/css/ >
[Accessed 4 June 2013]

Yoshioka, N., Washizaki, H., and Maruyama, K., (2008). A Survey on Security Patters: Progress in Informatics, No.5, pp35-47, (2008) PDF file special issue: The Future of Software Engineering for Security and Privacy [online] Available at < scholar.google.com/scholar?start=20&q=php+security+flaws&hl=en&as_sdt=0,5 >
[Accessed 30thJuly, 2013]

www.ingramcontent.com/pod-product-compliance
Lightning Source LLC
Chambersburg PA
CBHW051216050326

40689CB00008B/1330